Jean Partridge

POSITIVE
CHARGES

◆

544 Ways To Stay Upl
During Downbeat Ti

by Alexander Lockh

ZANDER
Z
PRESS

**Attention corporations, sales groups, colleges, universities,
and other organizations:**

This book may be purchased at bulk discount rates for use in educational
programs, as premiums in sales promotions or fund-raising campaigns.
Please contact the publisher.

First Printing October 1994
ISBN 0-9643035-5-8
Printed in the United States of America

To my family and friends who encouraged and supported me to live my dream. And to the loving memory of my father, who taught me that it's possible to shine through every adversity.

◆ INTRODUCTION ◆

For the most part, all my life I have been a happy person with a good positive mental attitude. I stated <u>for the most part</u> because it took me many years to understand the importance of finding true peace of mind and happiness. To me, this knowledge is the true definition of success. I also had to realize the importance of consistently working at developing and maintaining a positive mental attitude. I soon realized that my *attitude* was the single most powerful force I possessed.

In the following pages, I would like to share with you some of the positive affirmations and principles that have made a definite impact on my life. By applying these same principles, you too can immediately start building a more positive, winning attitude. I wish you the utmost happiness and success as you journey through life's many *positive* opportunities.

Alexander

According to a study by executive recruiters at Harvard University, 85 percent of everything a person accomplishes after university in the way of wealth, position, and status was the result of <u>attitude</u>; only 15 percent was the result of aptitude and abilities.

Allan Cox, author of *The Cox Report on the American Corporation*, found by surveying top executives of Fortune 500 companies, ninety-four percent of those surveyed attributed their success in life to <u>attitude</u> than any other single factor.

pos·i·tive (poz′ə·tiv) *adj.* Free from doubt or hesitation; confident; optimistic.

at·ti·tude (at′ə·tood) *n.* A way of acting or behaving that shows what one is thinking or feeling.

Choose your friends carefully.
A negative attitude is very
contagious and can rub off
on you little by little without
your knowledge.

1 ◆ Look forward, not backward.

2 ◆ Be a leader, not a follower.

3 ◆ Focus on your successes and learn from your failures.

4 ◆ Stay away from people who try to belittle your ambitions.

5 ◆ Trust your hopes, not your fears.

6 ◆ Go the extra mile at your job.

Attitude is Everything

Attitude is the way you think. Your attitude is something other people can actually see. They can hear it in your voice, see it in the way you move, and feel it when they are with you. Your attitude expresses itself in everything you do, all the time, wherever you are. Positive attitudes always invite positive results. Negative attitudes always invite negative results. Attitude makes a difference in everything you do for your entire life, every hour of every day. What you get out of each thing you do will equal the attitude you have when you do it.

Anything that you do with a positive attitude will work <u>for</u> you. Anything that you do with a negative attitude will work <u>against</u> you. If you have a positive attitude, you will look for ways to solve the problems that you can solve, and you will let go of the things over which you have no control.

You can develop a positive attitude by emphasizing the good, by being tough-minded, and by refusing defeat.

Anonymous

7 ◆ Develop high values.

8 ◆ Remember, you can if you think you can.

9 ◆ The biggest mistake you can make is to be afraid of making one.

10 ◆ Look at the challenges in life as stepping-stones to success.

11 ◆ If you want respect, have self-respect.

12 ◆ Act, don't react.

Humans can, by their thoughts and acts of will, considerably influence their feelings, health, and even their chemistry. This is the truth behind the effectiveness of positive thinking.

Donald Meyer

13 ◆ Start today and put your ideas into action.

14 ◆ Expect positive outcomes every day.

15 ◆ If what you're doing now isn't providing you with a sense of satisfaction, then *change* what you're doing.

16 ◆ Always look your best.

17 ◆ Finish what you start.

18 ◆ Learn to laugh at yourself.

Begin each day with a personal
outlook that will open doors,
welcome opportunity, and bring
serenity. Your attitude determines
your ability to experience success
and happiness.

19 ◆ Be consistent.

20 ◆ Determine what success really means to you. Then, put your thoughts in writing.

21 ◆ Analyze and evaluate the attitudes of current friends and associates.

22 ◆ Always have alternative plans.

23 ◆ Believe in yourself and what you are doing.

24 ◆ Focus your effort on constant achievement.

A Positive Mental Attitude urges you to:

- Seek the truth.
- Take constructive action.
- Strive to achieve the highest ideals you can conceive,
  consistent with good physical and mental health.
- Live intelligently in your society.
- Abstain from that which will cause unnecessary injury.
- Start from where you are and go to where you want to
  be regardless of what you are or what you have been.

Napoleon Hill

25 ◆ Do a little more each day than you think you possibly can.

26 ◆ Change the thoughts you hold in your mind, and change your life.

27 ◆ Be decisive.

28 ◆ Build a positive attitude of expectancy.

29 ◆ Refuse to be discouraged.

30 ◆ Don't try to win arguments.

By building and maintaining
a positive mental attitude,
you can achieve results you
never dreamed were possible.

31 ◆ Always find the best in people.

32 ◆ If you make up your mind you can't,
you'll always be right.

33 ◆ Remember that we first make our habits,
and then our habits make us.

34 ◆ Don't be afraid to be yourself.

35 ◆ Speak and write using positive words.

36 ◆ Open the door to new friends.

Whether a glass is half full or
half empty depends on the
attitude of the person
looking at it.

37 ◆ Build and develop your self-confidence.
Have faith in yourself.

38 ◆ Your future will be what you mentally
picture it to be.

39 ◆ Your life is a blackboard. Pick up the
chalk, and write out what you want.

40 ◆ Keep learning new things every day
of your life.

It is our attitude at the beginning of
a difficult undertaking which, more
than anything else, will determine
its successful outcome.

William James

41 ◆ Understand that you are your biggest competitor.

42 ◆ Don't sit back and take what comes. Go after what you want.

43 ◆ Help people to like themselves.

44 ◆ Stretch outside your comfort zone.

45 ◆ Resist the temptation to judge others.

46 ◆ Never surrender to external forces.

People can alter
their lives
by altering their
attitudes.

47 ◆ Believe in your own brilliance.

48 ◆ Build a reputation as a winner.

49 ◆ In order to change, you must be sick
and tired of being *sick and tired*.

50 ◆ Start out each day by focusing on the
positive aspects of your job.

51 ◆ Set aside time every day to daydream.

52 ◆ Expect big things from your life.

Our life is a
reflection of
our attitudes.

53 ◆ Be willing to accept occasional small setbacks.

54 ◆ Happiness doesn't depend on what you have; it depends on how you *feel* about what you have.

55 ◆ Try harder!

56 ◆ Stop wishing and start resolving.

57 ◆ Learn to act immediately upon a decision.

58 ◆ Keep raising your expectations.

You are the
sole master
of your attitude.

59 ◆ Begin and end each day with a
motivational self-talk.

60 ◆ Face fears head on.

61 ◆ Develop close relationships.

62 ◆ Take time out each day to give yourself
an attitude check.

63 ◆ Dare to aim high.

64 ◆ Keep your promises.

This may shock you, but I believe the single most significant decision I can make on a day-to-day basis is my choice of attitude. It is more important than my past, my education, my bankroll, my successes or failures, fame or pain, what other people think of me or say about me, my circumstances, or my position.

Attitude is that 'single string' that keeps me going or cripples my progress. It alone fuels my fire or assaults my hope. When my attitudes are right, there's no barrier too high, no valley too deep, no dream too extreme, no challenge too great for me. I am convinced that life is 10% what happens to me and 90% how I react to it. And so it is with you ... we are in charge of our attitudes.

Charles Swindoll

65 ◆ Learn to recognize signs of *tomorrow-itis*.

66 ◆ Make your mistakes. Learn from them. Move on.

67 ◆ What happens *in* you is more important than what happens *to* you.

68 ◆ Spend more time socializing.

69 ◆ Like what you do, and then do it well.

70 ◆ Learn to be a good listener.

Attitudes are much
more important
than aptitudes.

71 ◆ Stretch your imagination.

72 ◆ Learn to see the other person's viewpoint.

73 ◆ Give others your enthusiastic attention.

74 ◆ Take control of your attitude. Don't let someone else control it for you.

75 ◆ Be supportive to others and to the achievement of their goals.

76 ◆ Learn to improvise.

Attitude is the mind's
paint brush.
It can color any situation.

77 ◆ Keep your mind filled with thoughts of happiness, hope, peace, and courage.

78 ◆ Set aside time every day for solitude and reflection.

79 ◆ Understand there is only a letter difference between change and chance.

80 ◆ Make choices between being reactive and being creative.

Your living is determined not
so much by what life brings to
you as by the attitude you bring life.

John H. Miller

81 ◆ Do more for the world than the world does for you.

82 ◆ Be thankful for each day. Count your blessings instead of your problems.

83 ◆ Never believe you don't have what it takes.

84 ◆ Don't forget to laugh often.

85 ◆ Think before acting.

86 ◆ Seek happiness.

The good news is that the bad
news can be turned into
good news when you
change your attitude!

Robert H. Schuller

87 ◆ Learn to accept fair criticism without resentment.

88 ◆ Laugh with people and never at them.

89 ◆ Develop love where hate has been.

90 ◆ Recognize the inevitable.

91 ◆ Eliminate envy from your life.

92 ◆ Realize that your dreams of the future are better than the history of the past.

Let us think positively and remember that the misfortunes hardest to bear are those which rarely happen.

93 ◆ Don't look for faults, find remedies.

94 ◆ Develop your intuition.

95 ◆ Create a self-fulfilling prophecy of winning and success.

96 ◆ Take responsibility for your past, present, and future experiences.

97 ◆ If you don't know, say so.

98 ◆ Inspire others by your positive example.

A positive attitude is a state of
mind which is maintained each day
through optimism, enthusiasm,
and a belief in oneself and in
one's true potential.

99 ◆ Recognize the power of your thoughts
and increase the value of your ideas.

100 ◆ Avoid *Someday I'll* Syndrome.

101 ◆ Don't take the path of least resistance.

102 ◆ Realize that the biggest risk in life is
to do nothing.

103 ◆ Be forgiving toward others.

104 ◆ Always expect the unexpected.

Attitude is the
window through
which you must
see the world.

105 ◆ Get rid of the fear of failure.

106 ◆ Master your morale.

107 ◆ Believe that *If it's meant to be, it's up to me.*

108 ◆ Replace a negative habit with two positive habits.

109 ◆ Understand the choices you make today will shape your future.

110 ◆ Praise yourself every day.

Hardening of the attitudes
is the most deadly disease
on the face of the earth.

Zig Ziglar

111 ◆ Search for ways in which it can be done instead of looking for reasons it can't be done.

112 ◆ Stop studying your mistakes. Concentrate on studying your achievements and successes.

113 ◆ Ask yourself, "If I could do anything I wanted to do in life, what would it be?" Write it down and go for it!

114 ◆ Learn how to manage your time more effectively. Discipline yourself and eliminate procrastination.

Don't become addicted to
and dependent on negativism;
you may become a negaholic.

115 • Pursue life with a positive outlook.

116 • Be compassionate.

117 • Never condemn in others that which you see and know is in yourself.

118 • Stand up for what you believe.

119 • Tonight, look up at the stars.

120 • Don't let imaginary obstacles block you from getting what you want.

A positive mental attitude is the right
mental attitude for each specific
occasion. It has the power to
attract the good and the beautiful.
A negative attitude repels people and
will rob you of all that makes
life worth living.

Napoleon Hill

121 ◆ Be aware of the thoughts that occupy
your mind. Keep them positive.

122 ◆ Dedicate at least 30 minutes a day to
creative visualization.

123 ◆ Invest in yourself. That's where you'll
receive the best interest.

124 ◆ Recognize that you've had troubles before,
and you managed to survive them.

A positive attitude is not a
destination. It is a way
of life.

125 ◆ Seek out mentors and colleagues who will help you live your dreams.

126 ◆ Be a positive and aggressive listener.

127 ◆ Change worry time into planning time.

128 ◆ Spend this weekend doing something you really want to do.

129 ◆ Determine your values in life.

130 ◆ Admit your mistakes.

Attitudes are contagious.
Is yours worth catching?

131 ◆ Become a world-class prioritizer.

132 ◆ Take time to be friendly.

133 ◆ Recognize that your attitude is your most priceless possession.

134 ◆ Build a reputation for delivering more than you promised.

135 ◆ Control your temper.

136 ◆ Rise early. Work late. Strike oil. (J. Paul Getty)

Our only limitations are those
which we set up in our
minds or permit others
to establish for us.

Og Mandino

137 ◆ Develop positive behavior.

138 ◆ Listen to others and learn from them.

139 ◆ Devote some time to community support.

140 ◆ It is better to do something imperfectly
than to do nothing perfectly.

141 ◆ Learn to spot opportunities and seize
them courageously.

142 ◆ Take time out to enjoy the sunset.

It takes but one positive
thought, when given a chance
to survive and thrive, to overpower
an entire army of negative thoughts.

143 ◆ Help yourself by helping others.

144 ◆ Simplify your life.

145 ◆ Always strive to become the most knowledgeable person in your field.

146 ◆ Set up a target for your career and aim for it.

147 ◆ Follow your dominant desires.

148 ◆ Look to the future.

When we have accepted the worst,
we have nothing more to lose.
And that automatically means
we have everything to gain

Dale Carnegie

149 ◆ Concentrate on your assets, not
your limitations.

150 ◆ Keep an open mind.

151 ◆ Make amends with enemies.

152 ◆ Let your body language convey positive
things about you.

153 ◆ Work smarter, not harder.

154 ◆ Take pride in your work.

Your morning thoughts may determine your conduct for the day. Optimistic thoughts will make your day bright and productive, while pessimistic thinking will make it dull and wasteful.

Face each day cheerfully, smilingly, and courageously; and it will naturally follow that your work will be a real pleasure, and progress will be a delightful accomplishment.

William M. Peck

155 ◆ Replace fear with desire.

156 ◆ Always get a good night sleep.

157 ◆ Relinquish all excuses from your life.

158 ◆ Treat yourself as if you are the most important asset you will ever own.

159 ◆ Respect other people's opinions, even if they are different from your own.

160 ◆ Accept 100% responsibility for your life.

Remember: A positive attitude
produces a positive perception
and changes the situation
for the better.

161 ◆ Use your material gains in ways that
will benefit others.

162 ◆ Begin each day by planting positive
seeds of thought.

163 ◆ Welcome challenges, for they are the real
stimulators to success.

164 ◆ Take time to look at yourself through
other people's eyes.

We are all born with a
positive mental attitude.
We <u>learn</u> to be negative.

165 ◆ Avoid jumping to conclusions until you know all the facts.

166 ◆ Live your dreams, not someone else's.

167 ◆ Define your purpose in life. Write it down.

168 ◆ Invest a percentage of your annual income in personal and professional development.

169 ◆ Don't major in minor things.

170 ◆ Choose to love and be loved.

Positive thinking is the hope
that you can move mountains.
Positive believing is the same
hope, but with a reason for
believing you can do it.

171 ◆ Try smiling while using the phone.

172 ◆ Never think down, always think up.

173 ◆ Set aside a period of quietness each day.

174 ◆ Think only the best; work only for the best; expect only the best.

175 ◆ Make it a habit to give yourself credit for your accomplishments.

176 ◆ Listen for truth and speak the truth.

Ability is what you're capable of doing.
Motivation determines what you do.
Attitude determines how well you do it.

Lou Holtz

177 ◆ If you fail the first time, try again.

178 ◆ Strengthen your individuality.

179 ◆ Take charge of your thoughts instead
of allowing them to control you.

180 ◆ Picture in your mind the rewards that
will be yours when you reach your goals.

181 ◆ Live in the present.

182 ◆ Increase your spiritual understanding.

Conquer the *negative;*
explore the *positive.*

183 ◆ Make today count.

184 ◆ Keep improving your vocabulary.

185 ◆ Set aside some time each day for creative thinking.

186 ◆ Remind yourself that you are bigger than anything that can happen to you.

187 ◆ Act upon your ideas.

188 ◆ Be willing to admit when you've been wrong.

Your own mental attitude
is the one thing you possess
over which you alone
have complete control.

189 ◆ Always dress for success.

190 ◆ Celebrate your birthdays.

191 ◆ Avoid listening to gossip.

192 ◆ Overcome frustrations and irritations before they grow into big issues.

193 ◆ Learn not to dramatize the challenge you may be faced with.

194 ◆ Experiment with your versatility.

If you want to live positively,
you start by learning to
love <u>positively</u>.

Robert H. Schuller

195 ◆ When life hands you a lemon,
make lemonade.

196 ◆ Never judge a day by the weather.

197 ◆ Don't be an *if* thinker, be a *how* thinker.

198 ◆ Find a need and fill it.

199 ◆ Be sure your actions are consistent
with your communications.

200 ◆ Have vision.

Plant positive thoughts in
your mind and expect a
harvest of great possibilities.

201 ◆ Remember that you become what
you think about.

202 ◆ Discover your strengths and then use
them to the best advantage.

203 ◆ Understand that it's never too late to
change or achieve.

204 ◆ Take control of your life. Don't allow
circumstances to control you.

A friend of mine has a great attitude:
When something doesn't go his way,
instead of crying over spilt milk, he
just milks another cow!

205 ◆ Develop a *never-settle-for-defeat* attitude.

206 ◆ It's not where you are, it's where you go.

207 ◆ Join a social, religious, or service organization.

208 ◆ Spend more time with those you love.

209 ◆ Keep aiming to surpass your own best performance.

210 ◆ Be honest with yourself.

Your success, health, happiness,
and wealth can be attributed
to the choice of attitude.

211 ◆ Manage negativity.

212 ◆ To have courage, think courage.

213 ◆ Don't criticize, condemn or complain.

214 ◆ Adjust your attitude to accept things as they come if you cannot change or avoid them.

215 ◆ The way you see life will largely determine what you get out of it.

216 ◆ Avoid arguments.

BE POSITIVE;
then pass it on.

217 ◆ Believe that *"I can make a difference."*

218 ◆ Never let anyone shunt you from your aspirations.

219 ◆ Always see yourself as greater than you have ever been.

220 ◆ Remember that practice makes you <u>better</u>.

221 ◆ Go the extra mile.

222 ◆ Do things for the right reasons.

Plenty of people miss their share
of happiness, not because they
never found it, but because
they didn't stop to enjoy it.

W. Feather

223 • Listen to motivational audio tapes; read
books on success; and attend seminars
that will assist you in developing yourself.

224 • When you're feeling overwhelmed,
remember to take things one at a time—
one day at a time.

225 • Don't settle for less than your best. Aim
for excellence in your field and for constant
self-improvement.

226 • Implement small changes today,
and the result will be extraordinary
tomorrow.

A positive attitude
is an *inside* job.

227 ◆ Stop focusing on limiting beliefs.

228 ◆ Be grateful, not critical.

229 ◆ Believe that miracles can happen.

230 ◆ Remember that self-improvement
is a life-long process.

231 ◆ Be polite, courteous, and understanding
when dealing with people.

232 ◆ Project the image of a successful person.

Any fact facing us is not
as important as our attitude
toward it, for that determines
our success or failure.

Norman Vincent Peale

233 ◆ Set deadlines for yourself.

234 ◆ Avoid the negative suggestions of others.

235 ◆ Live with passion.

236 ◆ If you keep doing the same things, be prepared to get the same results.

237 ◆ Develop an attitude of gratitude.

238 ◆ Learn the art of conversation and make people feel at ease in your presence.

There is no danger of developing
eyestrain from looking on
the bright side of things.

239 ◆ Learn to react positively to negative situations.

240 ◆ Become self-reliant.

241 ◆ Don't waste other people's time.

242 ◆ Express the emotion of happiness instead of misery.

243 ◆ Commit your goals to writing.

244 ◆ Always look for a better way.

A positive mental attitude
combined with definiteness
of purpose is the starting
point of all worthwhile
achievement.

Napoleon Hill

245 • Cultivate good habits to weed out
bad habits.

246 • Develop a sincere desire for the things
you want in life.

247 • Use your initiative, your imagination,
and your ingenuity.

248 • Remove perfection from your vocabulary.
There's always room for improvement.

Thoughts, positive or negative,
grow stronger when fertilized
with constant repetition.

249 ◆ Build a reputation as a winner.

250 ◆ Refuse to set limitations on yourself.

251 ◆ Visualize yourself as the person you
want to be. (The me I see is the me I'll be.)

252 ◆ Keep your body in peak physical condition.
Physical fitness assures mental fitness.

253 ◆ Maintain a healthy diet.

254 ◆ Celebrate your victories.

One way to change
your attitude is to change
the way you think.

255 ◆ Make your first impression count.

256 ◆ Listen to your intuition.

257 ◆ Anticipate wonderful things happening to you each day.

258 ◆ Show understanding, sympathy, and a sincere interest in what others say.

259 ◆ Be willing to pay your dues.

260 ◆ Don't be <u>nosy</u>.

Positive attitudes
create positive people.

261 ◆ Eliminate doubt, despair, and other limitations from your mind.

262 ◆ Make your attitudes your allies.

263 ◆ Don't be afraid to spoil yourself.

264 ◆ Recognize that you deserve the very best in life and you can have it.

265 ◆ Pay your debts.

266 ◆ Never say never.

The positive mind has
extra solving power.

267 ◆ Aim above mediocrity.

268 ◆ Avoid negative thinkers.

269 ◆ Choose friends and associates compatible with your goals and interests.

270 ◆ The measure of success is living your life in your own way.

271 ◆ Stop magnifying your problems.

272 ◆ Say what's on your mind.

There is little difference in people...
the little difference is attitude.
The big difference is whether it
is positive or negative.

W. Clement Stone

273 ◆ Overcome shyness.

274 ◆ Eliminate your prejudices.

275 ◆ What goal would you pursue if you knew it was impossible to fail?

276 ◆ List the areas of your life in which you would like to become more disciplined.

277 ◆ Look at your present age positively.

278 ◆ Quit complaining.

Attitude is a habit
of thought.

279 ◆ Prepare to compromise.

280 ◆ If you don't know what you want in life,
a terrible thing happens—nothing.

281 ◆ Practice hope.

282 ◆ Show affection.

283 ◆ Don't allow someone's opinion of you
to become your reality.

284 ◆ Be a problem solver, not a problem maker.

Going the extra mile leads to
the development of a positive,
pleasing mental attitude, which
is essential for enduring success.

285 ◆ If you think you can or think you can't, you're right.

286 ◆ Train your mind to learn from your successes.

287 ◆ Remember that a person's name is the most pleasant sound to that person.

288 ◆ Hold your posture as if you were wearing a crown.

It isn't defeat, but your
mental attitude toward it,
that can whip you.

289 ◆ Share your talents in ways that will benefit others.

290 ◆ Keep on trying!

291 ◆ Sing at least one song every day.

292 ◆ Believe that you were born for greatness.

293 ◆ Overcome the negative tendency to think, "If only..."

294 ◆ Don't wait for opportunity, make it!

Positive attitudes
create a chain reaction
of positive thoughts.

295 ◆ Develop persistence.

296 ◆ Evaluate your current attitudes.

297 ◆ Set aside some time each week to spend with close friends.

298 ◆ Use the precious hours of each day wisely.

299 ◆ Every adversity carries with it the seeds of a greater benefit.

300 ◆ Never worship material things.

Take control of your
mental attitude;
keep it positive, and
you'll acquire the things
you want.

301 ◆ Never portray the role of defeat.

302 ◆ Never burn your bridges.

303 ◆ Adopt new behavior patterns that are
     consistent with whom you want to become.

304 ◆ Don't just love what you do, but become
     what you do.

305 ◆ Give compliments.

306 ◆ Trust your instincts.

A positive attitude won't let
you do anything. But it will let
you do everything better than a
negative attitude will.

Zig Ziglar

307 ♦ Stop putting yourself down.

308 ♦ What you conceive, if you believe, you will achieve.

309 ♦ Seek out positive, winning role models.

310 ♦ Plan purposefully, prepare prayerfully, proceed positively, pursue persistently.

311 ♦ Express yourself.

312 ♦ Develop a sense of urgency in your life.

Make a positive attitude your daily habit.

313 • Remember to say, "Thank you."

314 • Make a commitment to control those things you say when you talk to yourself.

315 • Be flexible.

316 • Save 10 percent of what you earn.

317 • Find a friend who has the gift of encouragement.

318 • Live life rather than letting life live you.

The most significant
decision you can make
on a day-to-day basis is
the choice of your attitude.

319 ◆ Don't conform to the norm.

320 ◆ Always have something to look forward to.

321 ◆ Change possibilities to probabilities.

322 ◆ Try to learn and eventually profit
from your losses.

323 ◆ Fly with the eagles, don't scratch with
the turkeys.

324 ◆ Completely relax your body, part by part.

Your attitude determines
your altitude.

325 ◆ Build a radiant, cheerful, and
optimistic personality.

326 ◆ Give yourself positive suggestions
throughout the day.

327 ◆ Ability is important, dependability
is critical.

328 ◆ Write down your thoughts on a
regular basis.

When you realize that the worst
that can happen is that you may
have to face a disappointment,
then you will be transformed from
a doubter to a believer, from a
negative thinker to a
<u>positive thinker</u>.

329 ◆ Be the master of your moods.

330 ◆ Never give others the responsibility
for your happiness.

331 ◆ Don't let the negativity of others
pull you down.

332 ◆ Get rid of that guilt complex.

333 ◆ Practice patience.

334 ◆ Keep it simple.

When you maintain a
positive mental attitude,
the problems of your
world tend to bow
before you.

335 ◆ Never compare yourself with other people
nor your achievements with theirs; instead,
make your comparisons only with yourself.

336 ◆ Always affirm to yourself that there
is a solution to any problem and
that you can find it.

337 ◆ Wake up each day and tell yourself that
it's going to be a great day, and look forward
to each hour with enthusiasm.

338 ◆ Appreciate life. It gives you the
chance to love and to work and to
play and to look at the stars.

A positive attitude is like a fire:
Unless you continue to add fuel,
it goes out.

339 ◆ Get rid of regret.

340 ◆ Practice the art of appreciation.

341 ◆ Be open to new ideas, relationships, and experiences.

342 ◆ Train your mind to see and accept opportunity.

343 ◆ Stay focused.

344 ◆ Don't nurse a grudge.

A positive attitude
attracts happiness.

A negative attitude
repels happiness.

345 ◆ Eliminate fear— **F**alse **E**vidence
Appearing **R**eal.

346 ◆ Practice what you preach.

347 ◆ Remember, we tend to get what we expect.

348 ◆ Think confidently by acting confidently.

349 ◆ Treat yourself to something that will help
you feel good and put a smile on your face.

350 ◆ Don't be egotistical.

Attitude is a little thing
that makes a BIG difference.

351 ◆ Look for the sunshine behind every dark cloud.

352 ◆ Say hello to everyone.

353 ◆ Don't go through life on <u>automatic pilot.</u>

354 ◆ Surround yourself with positive, supportive, quality people.

355 ◆ Learn not to brag.

356 ◆ Plan your day.

If you want to see the rainbow,
you have to be willing to
put up with a little rain.

357 • Keep a journal or diary to track your
progress, and review your goals.

358 • Be open to your true feelings.

359 • Respond positively to negative feedback.

360 • Don't be afraid to ask for help or
guidance when you need it.

361 • Avoid being lazy.

362 • Maintain a *keep-it-going* attitude.

You can't always control the
circumstances in life, but you
can control your attitude toward
those circumstances.

363 ◆ Remember, every problem has a
limited life span.

364 ◆ Astonish yourself!

365 ◆ Don't go through life with your mental
parking brake on. Release your brakes!

366 ◆ No matter what others think, go forward.

367 ◆ Walk your talk.

368 ◆ To be a success, you have to <u>stand</u> <u>out</u>.

Nothing great was
ever achieved without a
positive mental attitude.

369 ◆ Never allow your problems to become
the centerpiece of your conversations.

370 ◆ Master your emotions; don't let them
master you.

371 ◆ Remember that every improvement is
a *big* improvement.

372 ◆ Don't wait for your ship to come in;
swim out to it.

In an organization, doing is causing
people to have a productivity that makes
everything happen on time and profitably.
The attitude of doing comes from the
leader's attitude.

Philip B. Crosby

373 ◆ Make a decision to raise your standards.

374 ◆ Take counsel from your beliefs, not your fears.

375 ◆ Never, never, never give up. Act as if it were impossible to fail.

376 ◆ Respect others.

377 ◆ Forgive yourself for past mistakes.

378 ◆ Take ownership of your reputation.

Defeat may be a stepping-stone
or a stumbling block depending
on whether your attitude is
positive or negative.

379 ◆ Know when to say no.

380 ◆ No rule of success will work if you don't.

381 ◆ Adjust your attitude and behavior to be a 110% person.

382 ◆ Explore your hobbies and favorite pastimes.

383 ◆ You can always turn setbacks into comebacks with a positive mental attitude.

384 ◆ Do a lot of little things.

The meaning of things lies not
in the things themselves, but in
our attitude toward them.

Stuart Gilbert

385 ◆ Smile, it takes only 13 muscles.
A frown takes 112.

386 ◆ Focus on what you want in life, and
don't let anyone stand in your way.

387 ◆ Celebrate life.

388 ◆ Organize yourself. Use a daily planner.

389 ◆ Don't become a *spilt-milk* worrier.

390 ◆ Be rational.

391 ◆ Avoid dependence on drugs, alcohol, and tobacco.

392 ◆ Follow your heart.

393 ◆ Face today's challenge fearlessly and prepare for the future.

394 ◆ Eliminate self-destructive behavior.

395 ◆ Take a course in public speaking.

396 ◆ Tell your friends that you appreciate them.

I think it is absolutely
essential that you have a
positive mental attitude in every
aspect of life and that you start early.

Patrick O'Malley

397 ◆ When you can't solve a problem, manage it.

398 ◆ Act enthusiastically, for as you act you tend to be.

399 ◆ Be willing to make sacrifices to get opportunities.

400 ◆ Always try to be fair.

401 ◆ Ability x Effort = Results.

402 ◆ Know your limits.

A positive thinker does not
refuse to recognize the negative;
he refuses to dwell on it.

403 ◆ Avoid feelings of inferiority.

404 ◆ Never take life for granted.

405 ◆ Take time to write out a success inventory
of yourself. Ask yourself, "What have I
accomplished this far in life?"

406 ◆ Don't worry about tomorrow.

407 ◆ Take time to relax.

408 ◆ Do your best with what you have.

A positive thinker learns
to knock the "t" off the "can't."

409 ◆ Remove yourself from an environment
that you don't like or is causing you pain.

410 ◆ Think and act cheerfully, and you
will feel cheerful.

411 ◆ Positive anything is better than
negative nothing.

412 ◆ Never underestimate the repellent power
of a negative attitude.

A positive attitude is the
one characteristic that all
successful people have in common.

413 ◆ Dare to take a chance.

414 ◆ Get interested in your neighbors.

415 ◆ Begin getting in the habit of <u>doing it now.</u>

416 ◆ You get out of life what you expect. So don't resign yourself to your present role in life.

417 ◆ Get up an hour earlier in the morning.

418 ◆ Cultivate a good sense of humor.

With a good attitude, we can
turn negative experiences
into positive lessons.

419 ◆ Always make everyone feel better
because of you.

420 ◆ Be more curious.

421 ◆ Beware of negative thinking experts.

422 ◆ Learn not to put a stopwatch on
advancement.

423 ◆ Handle your money wisely.

424 ◆ Celebrate your victories.

Be a positive thinker,
not an <u>if</u> thinker.

425 ◆ Dare to be original.

426 ◆ Make a strong commitment to reach your full potential as a human being.

427 ◆ Use common sense.

428 ◆ Act positively, and you will become positive.

429 ◆ Write out a list of ten things you like about yourself, and review it each day.

430 ◆ Never verbalize a negative emotion.

Attitude is the first quality that marks a successful person. If a person has a positive attitude and is a positive thinker who likes challenges and difficult situations, then half of their success is achieved.

On the other hand, if a person is a negative thinker who is narrow-minded and refuses to accept new ideas and has a defeatist attitude, they haven't got a chance.

Lowell Peacock

431 ◆ Read books on self-improvement, and start building your mental library.

432 ◆ Be a future-tense person.

433 ◆ Don't be afraid of sentiment.

434 ◆ Decide to let go of something that's been eating at you.

435 ◆ Practice positive expectations.

436 ◆ Let your desires become your obsession.

The outer conditions of a
person's life will always be
found to reflect their inner beliefs.

James Allen

437 ◆ Keep a weekly *"to do"* list.

438 ◆ Be tactful.

439 ◆ Don't allow past sorrows to become present emotions.

440 ◆ Cultivate faith in the future and confidence in yourself.

441 ◆ Expect more of yourself.

442 ◆ Become aware of your negative thinking.

Our attitude can be
the anchor of the soul,
the stimulus to action,
and the incentive to achievement.

443 ◆ Constantly set new goals.

444 ◆ Refuse to believe when someone says,
"It can't be done."

445 ◆ Create your own fortunes.

446 ◆ Decide what you want most to achieve.

447 ◆ Avoid people who point out your
faults all the time.

448 ◆ Learn to separate facts from fiction.

Our attitude toward the world around us depends upon what we are ourselves. If we are selfish, we will be suspicious of others. If we are of a generous nature, we will be likely to be more trustful. If we are quite honest with ourselves, we won't always be anticipating deceit in others. If we are inclined to be fair, we won't feel that we are being cheated. In a sense, looking at the people around you is like looking in the mirror. You see a reflection of yourself.

Anonymous

449 ◆ Believe that there is no circumstance stronger than your desire to accomplish your true purpose.

450 ◆ Write down on paper, "I'm going to do the following tomorrow." Then, fill in your own one-day program.

451 ◆ Ask, and it shall be given to you; seek, and you shall find; knock, and it shall be opened unto you. (Matthew 7:7-8)

452 ◆ Today, do something specific that will demonstrate your determination to change yourself and your life for the better.

You can think negatively
or positively. If you are a
positive thinker, you will base your
decisions on faith rather than fear.

Robert H. Schuller

453 ◆ Try to look for the positive when faced
with negative situations.

454 ◆ Each day, collect and review quotes that
motivate and inspire you.

455 ◆ Avoid all negative thoughts, and replace
them with positive affirmations.

456 ◆ Stay focused on your goals and objectives,
no matter what.

A positive mind finds
a way it can be done.

A negative mind looks for
all the ways it can't be done.

457 ◆ Start early each day.

458 ◆ Stop feeling sorry for yourself.

459 ◆ Remove yourself from toxic, unhealthy relationships.

460 ◆ Write out your worries on paper, then tear it up and throw it away.

461 ◆ Stick to your New Year's resolutions.

462 ◆ Work toward progress, not perfection.

Nothing can stop the man with the right mental attitude from achieving his goals; nothing on earth can help the man with the wrong mental attitude.

W. W. Ziege

463 ◆ Keep secrets secret.

464 ◆ Avoid being cold, cruel, and calculating.

465 ◆ Laugh when the going gets rough.
It releases your tensions.

466 ◆ All things are possible to him who
believeth. (Mark 9:23)

467 ◆ Always be on time.

468 ◆ Learn not to equate money with success.

The greatest discovery of my
generation is that human beings,
by changing the inner attitude
of their minds, can change
the outer aspects of their lives.

William James

469 ◆ Approach everyone you meet today with
       a sincere smile, friendliness, and a
       positive attitude.

470 ◆ Free yourself from false beliefs.

471 ◆ Be considerate.

472 ◆ Accept change as inevitable.

473 ◆ Have confidence in your judgement.

474 ◆ Know thyself.

Personal deficiencies might be termed negative qualities and include unreliability, failure to cooperate, laziness, untidiness, trouble making, interference, and dishonesty.

Positive qualities would include willingness, cheerfulness, courtesy, honesty, neatness, reliability, and temperance.

Many fail in their work because they are unable to overcome one personal deficiency. Check up on yourself. Don't be afraid to put yourself under a microscope.

Eliminate your negative qualities. Develop your positive ones. You can't win with the check mark in the wrong place.

M. Winette

475 ◆ Be a friend to yourself.

476 ◆ Never say, "I can't."

477 ◆ Don't be afraid to change jobs to find the work you would truly like to do.

478 ◆ Discover obvious and unrecognized time wasters. Develop your time awareness.

479 ◆ Learn from the past, but don't live there.

480 ◆ Be lenient with yourself.

Research has demonstrated that a
positive attitude can strengthen the
immune system, ward off illness,
help fight disease, and influence
healing and recovery from
long-term illness.

481 ◆ Try to be more spontaneous.

482 ◆ Live each day as fully as you can.

483 ◆ Start taking the necessary actions
to become the person you want to be.

484 ◆ Make people around you feel needed.

485 ◆ Surround yourself with *"can-do"* people.

486 ◆ Do something each day that you do well
no matter how insignificant it may seem.

Developing a positive
mental attitude will help
you create a positive life.

487 ◆ Use more of your potential.

488 ◆ Be flexible.

489 ◆ Give a helping hand and support to
someone who is faced with a challenge
of feeling down and out.

490 ◆ Be assertive.

491 ◆ When you're wrong, admit it.

492 ◆ Look forward to the unknown.

Real optimism sees the
negatives but
accentuates the positive.

William Arthur Ward

493 ◆ Develop attitudes that will get you
what you want.

494 ◆ Accentuate the positive, eliminate
the negative.

495 ◆ Don't hold back. Let others know
how you feel.

496 ◆ Think about what you can do for others,
not what they can do for you.

The attitudes of your friends
are like the buttons on an elevator.
They will either take you up or
they will take you down.

497 ◆ Support charities.

498 ◆ Take one step at a time.

499 ◆ Always be prepared for opportunity.

500 ◆ You can have anything you want if you will give up the belief that you can't.

501 ◆ Transform positive thinking into positive action.

502 ◆ Think, "I'm a winner"; not, "I'm a loser."

A positive attitude is like
a bank account. You can't
continually draw on it without
making deposits.

Wolf J. Rinke

503 ◆ Set specific goals.

504 ◆ Transcend old beliefs and limitations.

505 ◆ Eliminate from your vocabulary "*could've*," "*would've*" and "*should've*."

506 ◆ Spend at least 30 minutes a day reading something that is positive and inspirational.

507 ◆ Be realistic.

508 ◆ Always be excited.

The word "attitude" has taken on a new, more restrictive meaning, usually with the connection of "bad attitude" as in "I sense in you an attitude" or "The meeting was charged with an attitude."

Expanding the word into its older, more useful meaning of a general show of one's disposition, I think that we can explore the concept of attitude in a fruitful way. Attitude is the first face we show to the outside world. It can be physical, as in "body language." If my whole body is leaning toward the door, it shows clearly how much I want out of a boring or upsetting circumstance. Again, in some mysterious way our inner attitude radiates a meaning easily read.

Our attitudes betray our most secret thoughts and emotions. No matter how we try to hide them, they leak out somehow and display us with all the gross openness of an anatomical chart. Sometimes if we look at them carefully enough, they can reveal things about us that we ourselves were not aware of. We can make our attitudes an important tool of self-knowledge. It's a face we may or may not like, but it's one that's always with us. And yes, when we know our attitudes, we can change them.

Edward J. Lavin, S.J.

509 ◆ Make enthusiasm your daily habit.

510 ◆ Don't be an <u>other-people</u> blamer.

511 ◆ Free yourself from nervousness and tension.

512 ◆ Expect the best from yourself and others.

513 ◆ Banish loneliness and depression.

514 ◆ Make up a schedule for tomorrows work before you go to bed tonight.

A positive mental attitude not
only helps you visualize what you
want to be, it helps you become it.

Wally Amos

515 • You never can enhance the skills of
your outer world until you enhance
the skills of your inner world.

516 • Make a list of all the things you wish to
change. Acknowledge those things you
can't change, and take action upon those
things you can.

517 • As a man thinks within himself, so
he is. (Proverbs 23:)

518 • Write out on paper an honest self-appraisal.
Take stock of your abilities and
special talents.

What is an attitude?

It is the 'advance man' of our true selves.
Its roots are inward, but its fruit is outward.
It is our best friend or our worst enemy.
It is more honest and more consistent than our words.
It is an outward look based on past experiences.
It is a thing which draws people to us or repels them.
It is never content until it is expressed.
It is the librarian of our past.
It is the speaker of our present.
It is the prophet of our future.

John Maxwell

519 ◆ Take the *should's* in life and make
them *must's.*

520 ◆ Spend your money wisely.

521 ◆ Make habits work for you, not against you.

522 ◆ Avoid making the same mistake twice.

523 ◆ Build your reputation and values for
honesty, integrity, and passion.

524 ◆ Keep busy.

The pleasure you get from your
life is equal to the attitude
you put into it.

525 ◆ Concentrate on foresight, and forget hindsight.

526 ◆ Give and give when it isn't expected.

527 ◆ Remember, if you want to change your life, you have to *change your life!*

528 ◆ Improve your ability to easily persuade others.

529 ◆ Treat others as you want them to treat you.

530 ◆ One final word about criticism — *don't.*

The Optimist Creed:

Promise Yourself -

- To be so strong that nothing can disturb your peace of mind.
- To talk health, happiness and prosperity to every person you meet.
- To make all your friends feel that there is something in them.
- To look at the sunny side of everything and make your optimism come true.
- To think only the best, to work only for the best and expect only the best.
- To be just as enthusiastic about the success of others as you are about your own.
- To forget the mistakes of the past and press on to the greater achievements of the future.
- To give so much time to the improvement of yourself that you have no time to criticize others.
- To be too large for worry, too noble for anger, too strong for fear, and too happy to permit the presence of trouble.

Source: The Optimist Clubs of America

531 ◆ The secret to getting things done is
to take action.

532 ◆ When things become so bad that they
cannot become worse, they usually
begin to get better.

533 ◆ Believe that life is worth living, and your
belief will help create the fact. (William James)

534 ◆ Stop letting someone else make decisions
for you. Make them yourself.

Things are for us only what we
hold them to be. Which is to say that
our attitude toward things is more likely
in the long run to be more important
than the things themselves.

A.W. Tozer

535 ◆ Eliminate boredom, create excitement.

536 ◆ Work on improving your memory skills.

537 ◆ Insist on respect. If you give it, you
will receive it.

538 ◆ Listen to upbeat and inspiring music.

539 ◆ Before going to bed, flush the bad
emotions out of your mind.

540 ◆ Put your problems in their proper perspective.

A bad attitude is the worst thing
that can happen to a group of
people. It's infectious.

Wall Street Journal
April 1984

541 ◆ Never forget that your present does not
limit your future.

542 ◆ Make a list of the things you want
in life.

543 ◆ Develop the habit of thinking about things
constructively in order to improve them.

544 ◆ Give something away daily - a hug,
compliment, gift, etc...

⇨ Reread this book.

Positive thinking is how you
think about a problem.
Enthusiasm is how you *feel*
about a problem.
The two together determine
what you *do* about a problem.

POSITIVE SELF-TALK

Few of us realize the tremendous amount of influence that our thoughts and inner monologue have on helping us in life or preventing us from succeeding in life. The thoughts that occupy our minds, and what we say when we talk to ourselves (our self-talk) become our reality if dwelled upon or repeated often enough. Your mind believes what you tell it most. So it's important to teach yourself to think and talk with a positive dialogue.

One of the most powerful ways to build a more positive, winning attitude is through the continuous use of positive affirmation. An affirmation is a positive, goal-oriented statement spoken with conviction to yourself in the first person. Affirmations (or autosuggestions) are based on the way you would like things to be. They are stated as if the goal or desire has already been achieved. The use of positive affirmations means developing a habit of replacing negative messages with positive reinforcements. As these positive messages become part of your subconscious, they will soon be brought into your reality.

You must change what you say in order to change what you see. In order for your affirmations to be fully effective, they must have the following attributes:

1) They must be personal. For example, use the "I am", "I do", and "I will" statements.

2) They must be positive. Affirmations must be positive statements and should affirm what you are moving toward, not away from.

3) They must be in the present tense. Don't use words like "someday" or "soon".

4) They must be specific. For example, instead of saying, "I will make a lot of money" say, "I make_____amount of dollars per year".

5) They must be believable. You must believe in yourself and your abilities. Don't set your aim so high that you can't imagine or accept what you want to accomplish.

Along with creating your own personal affirmations, here are some positive statements you can use that will help you eliminate negative thought patterns and will produce changes in your attitude and outlook on life. Over the next 21 days repeat these statements to yourself once in the morning and once at night before retiring. You can also write them out on index cards and review them several times throughout the day:

1 ◆ I believe something wonderful is going to happen to me today.

2 ◆ I am a lovable, worthwhile person capable of caring for others.

3 ◆ I am a special person.

4 ◆ Because of my positive attitude, people are attracted to me.

5 ◆ I am a positive, exciting person to know. I am great fun to be around.

6 ◆ I write out my goals each day. I know exactly what I want.

7 ◆ I have a lot to be happy about.

8 ◆ I am becoming a more positive, happy person every single day.

9 ◆ I am a source of unlimited personal power. I control my destiny.

10 ◆ I have made a positive decision to succeed.

11 ◆ I enthusiastically welcome life's challenges with a positive attitude.

12 ◆ I fill my mind with positive reinforcements each day.

13 ◆ I choose to see the best in people and to share my optimistic outlook with them.

14 ◆ I am in control, and calm under all circumstances.

15 ◆ I turn problems and adversities into opportunities.

16 ◆ I wake up each day with a positive attitude and expect the best.

17 • I accept those risks necessary to achieve positive fulfillment of my goals.

18 • I maintain a balance of positive thoughts, feelings, and images in my mind.

19 • I deal successfully with difficult and negative people.

20 • I am a loving, forgiving person.

21 • I am a <u>do-it-now</u> person.

22 • I see myself as a strong and healthy person.

23 • I can identify and control stress in my life.

24 • I am in control of my financial success.

25 • I am a very creative person with a powerful imagination.

26 ◆ I deserve the best.

27 ◆ I can control procrastination in my life.

28 ◆ I am a winner whose life is a positive, exciting adventure.

29 ◆ I can do and accomplish anything I desire.

30 ◆ I am in charge of my ability to accomplish my goals and live my dreams.

31 ◆ _____

32 ◆ _____

33 ◆ _____

34 ◆ _____

35 ◆ _____

Take time right now to fill in your personal commitment and review it each day.

My Personal Commitment

I,_____, am hereby committed to building and maintaining a positive, winning attitude for myself and toward others. As of today, I will strive for excellence, write out my goals each day, and eliminate all negative thinking and influences in my life.

I promise that I will take the necessary steps to create a positive environment and develop my personal positive power to its fullest. I alone control and take personal ownership of my attitude, and I am committed to making each day a great day. I am a positive, winning person who believes in my ability to overcome any challenge that I face.

_____
Signature

To help me stay positively charged I will

Practice maintaining a positive attitude each day.

Occupy my mind with motivational monologue.

Set and implement realistic goals.

Isolate negative thinking and influences.

Take control and conquer my fears.

Identify and eliminate stress.

Visualize my success.

Expect the best from each day.

The Choice Is Yours!

In my many contacts with people, I have come to the conclusion that there are two kinds of people and two types of attitudes that will determine a person's success or failure in life. The first example includes people who are very happy with themselves and with life. They have a positive attitude and a very positive outlook. These positive people are optimistic; they have positive expectations; they take the necessary actions to produce the desired results; and they are very confident in themselves. They are also very outgoing, unselfish, enthusiastic, respectful, and pleasant to be around.

The other example includes people who are very unhappy with themselves and with the challenges that confront them. Not only are these people unhappy, but they also seem to have a negative attitude toward life. I call them negaholics. I have found that these negative people are fully occupied by anger and resentment. They are the first to criticize others. They seem to often worry, procrastinate, and live in fear of failure. They luxuriate in self-pity and depression. They are more worried about changing others than changing themselves.

Think about these examples for a moment—happy, positive people and unhappy, negative people. Which of these two examples best describes your current mental state and actions? Which one would you like to subscribe to from now on? Great, I knew you were committed to building a positive, winning attitude for yourself and toward others. Now go out there and let that attitude make it happen!

With the right attitude, all the problems in the world will not make you a failure. With the wrong mental attitude, all the help in the world will not make you a success.

Warren Deaton

Personal
Action Planner

Determine what success really means to you.

Each one of us has a different way of defining success in our own life. Maybe you define it by your achievements or by your possessions. What steps can you take today that will make you feel more successful? What is missing in your life that is keeping you from feeling fulfilled? Write down your definition based on what you expect from yourself.

My personal definition of success:

_____

_____

_____

_____

Define your purpose in life.

What would you like to have, do, or become in life? What is the one thing that you want to achieve that will enrich you as a person and give your life meaning? Begin building the foundation for a fulfilling future by writing down your true desire.

My purpose is:

_____

_____

_____

_____

_____

Commit your goals to writing.
(A goal that is not written down is merely a wish.)

Below, write down the things that you want to achieve or accomplish in life. Even if you don't know exactly what you want, don't let that keep you from filling it in. Your goals will tend to come to you and become more clear as you put them down on paper. When you have finished, write out an immediate action (no matter how small) you can take that will bring you closer to what you want. Review your list 3 times a day.

Here are my goals: Immediate action:

1) _____   _____

2) _____   _____

3) _____   _____

4) _____   _____

Write out on paper an honest self-appraisal.
Take stock of your abilities and special talents.

Each one of us is blessed with specific talents that make us unique as a person. You may have musical talents, artistic abilities, or good communication skills. Don't sell yourself short. There is something that you do well, no matter how insignificant you may feel it is. Try not to concentrate on the things you can't do, but look at the things you can do. Write out some of these special talents, and give yourself the praise that you deserve.

My special talents include:

_____   _____

_____   _____

_____   _____

_____   _____

Write out your worries on paper then, tear
it up and throw it away.

It has been said that 40 percent of the things we worry about
never happen; 30 percent of the things we worry about we can't
change; 12 percent of our worries are about health; 10 percent of
our time spent worrying is on petty and miscellaneous things; and
8 percent of our worry time is on real problems. Therefore 92
percent of the things we worry about can be avoided. Take time
now to list out those things that are bothering you. Ask yourself,
"Do I need to spend my time worrying about this?" "What specific
action can I take that will eliminate the challenge that I'm faced
with?"

Worry List:

_____

_____

_____

After you have written down your worries, check off those that may be unnecessary.
Then, mentally tear them from the page, and throw them away!

Write out a list of ten things you like about
yourself, and review it each day.

Sometimes we fail to recognize just how great and unique we really
are. Low self-esteem begins with focusing on those certain things
that you wish you could change about yourself. But what about
all of your special gifts, abilities, and talents? Don't be modest.
List your good qualities. You are an extraordinary human being,
and you should be proud!

Things I like about myself:

1) _____   6) _____

2) _____   7) _____

3) _____   8) _____

4) _____   9) _____

5) _____   10) _____

List the areas of your life in which you would
like to become more disciplined.

What are some areas in your life that you need to improve on? Are
you disorganized? Always running a little late? Do you procrastinate? Would you like to maintain your ideal weight? List six
things and make a commitment to work on improving them. You
may discover that these areas could be causing you unwanted
stress and discomfort.

Areas I need to improve:

1) _____

2) _____

3) _____

4) _____

5) _____

6) _____

Dear Friend,

Thank you! I sincerely hope that my book will help you understand the power of maintaining an optimistic outlook toward your future. Each one of us contains the power to achieve greatness, and you hold the key to your destiny. Rekindle the fire in you; dare to dream; take action that will change your life in some positive way; and remember that life is like an elevator. It will sometimes take you up, and sometimes down. But, if you maintain a positive, winning attitude, you will always reach the top. Please let me know how you're doing. I will be delighted to hear from you. Also, if you have any suggestions or your own perils of wisdom that you would like to share with me, please send them to me. I might use them in my next book.

Alezach Talbit

C\O Zander Press
P.O. Box 11741
Richmond, VA. 23230

Bottom Liners

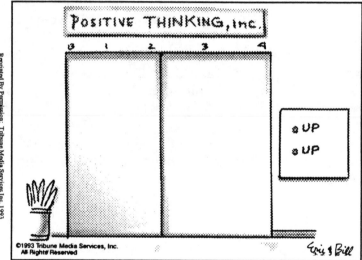

Order Form

Would you like additional copies of this book? <u>Positive Charges</u>
<u>(544 Ways To Stay Upbeat During Downbeat Times)</u> makes a great
gift for friends. Each book is $6.95 plus $2.00 for postage and
handling. (Virginia residents must include 4 1\2% state sales tax.)
Please allow 2 weeks for delivery. Send check payable to

Zander Press
P.O. Box 11741
Richmond, Virginia 23230

Also available on audio cassette: <u>STEPS TOWARD BUILDING A</u>
<u>POSITIVE ATTITUDE</u>

$9.95
(plus $2.00 shipping)

A 60 minute program
that will unlock your
Personal Positive Power!